50

fantastic things to do with
Toddlers

SALLY AND PHILL FEATHERSTONE

GH10047 | A Gryphon House Book

Parenting

50 Fantastic Things to Do With Toddlers

Gryphon House, Inc. Lewisville, NC

SALLY AND PHILL FEATHERSTONE

50 FANTASTIC THINGS TO DO WITH TODDLERS

by Sally and Phill Featherstone

COPYRIGHT

© 2013 Bloomsbury Publishing PLC
Published by Gryphon House, Inc. P.O. Box 10, Lewisville, NC 27023
800.638.0928 (phone); 877.638.7576 (fax).
Visit us on the web at www.gryphonhouse.com

Originally published in 2010 by A&C Black Publishers Limited.

Reprinted August 2014

LIBRARY OF CONGRESS

CATALOGING-IN-PUBLICATION INFORMATION

Featherstone, Sally.
 50 fantastic things to do with toddlers / by Sally and Phill Featherstone.
    pages cm
 "Originally published in 2010 by A&C Black Publishers Limited"--Publisher's note.
 Includes index.
 ISBN 978-0-87659-465-0
 1. Toddlers--Development. 2. Education, Preschool--Parent participation 3.
 Education, Preschool--Activity programs. 4. Play. I. Featherstone, Phill. II. Title. III.
 Title: Fifty fantastic things to do with toddlers.
 HQ774.5.F433 2013
 372.21--dc23
                          2012044470

Contents

Introduction

There's plenty of research to show that babies and children who enjoy a stimulating home environment learn better and more quickly. So, what parents and caregivers do to lay the groundwork for learning early on is an investment that pays back throughout the child's life.

This book has been written especially for parents to use with their young children at home. However, it can also be used by caregivers and workers in daycare and child care settings. It contains 50 simple activities that can be done easily with very little equipment, often in your spare time. It's not a course to work through. All the ideas here are suitable for babies from 16–36 months, and in many cases beyond. Some are more suited to younger babies and some to older. It's obvious which these are. Choose what you and your child enjoy. When you find an activity you like, do it again and again. Children love repetition and benefit from it.

There are three books in the 50 Fantastic Things series:

50 Fantastic Things to Do with Babies (suitable for use from soon after birth to 20 months)
50 Fantastic Things to Do with Toddlers (suitable for use from 16–36 months)
50 Fantastic Things to Do with Preschoolers (suitable for use from 30–50 months)

The age groupings above are approximate and are only suggestions. Children develop at different speeds. They also grow in spurts, with some periods of rapid development alternating with other times when they don't seem to change as quickly. So, don't worry if your baby doesn't seem ready for a particular activity. Try another instead, and return to it later. On the other hand, if your baby gets on well and quickly, try some of the ideas in the "Another idea" and "Ready for more?" sections.

Finally, please remember that one of the main aims of this book is fun. There are few things as delightful or rewarding as being alongside young children as they explore, inquire, experiment, and learn. Join them in their enthusiasm for learning and enjoy being with them!

A NOTE ON SAFETY

Care must be taken at all times when dealing with toddlers and young children. Common sense will be your main guide, but here are a few ideas to help you have fun safely:

Toddlers and young children naturally explore things by bringing them to their mouths. This is fine, but always check that toys and other objects you use are clean.

Although rare, swallowing objects or choking on them is a hazard. Some children are more susceptible than others. If you are concerned about choking, buy a choking tester from a retail baby-supply store.

A child's lungs are delicate. They need clean air. Never smoke near your child, and don't allow anyone else to do so.

Children are naturally inquisitive, and you will want to encourage this. However, secure and happy children are often unaware of danger. Your toddler needs you to watch out for him. Make sure you are always there. You can't watch your toddler all the time, but don't leave him alone and unsupervised for more than a few minutes at a time. Even when he is asleep, check on him regularly.

The objects and toys we suggest here have been chosen for their safety.Nevertheless, most things can be dangerous if they go wrong or are not used properly:

- Mobiles and toys tied to baby gyms are great to encourage looking and reaching, but check that they are fastened securely.
- Ribbons and string are fascinating to children, but they can be a choking hazard. They can also become wrapped around arms, legs, and necks.
- Toddlers are natural explorers. They need clean floors. Store outdoor shoes away from areas where your toddler will be walking and crawling.
- If your toddler is just learning to balance, either sitting or standing, make sure she has a soft landing. If your toddler is starting to walk, look out for trip hazards.
- Take care with furniture. Make sure your toddler is fastened securely into her high chair. Pad sharp edges of tables and other furniture.

7

What is your child learning?

This is important for learning to identify objects and naming them, as well as for developing the concept of sharing

Over to You
giving and taking

DID YOU KNOW?

Interactions with other people stimulate brain growth in young children—this helps learning.

WHAT YOU NEED:

- a basket of everyday objects (for example: brushes, sponges, plastic cups, wooden spoons, rattles, and so on)

Ready for more?

If your baby seems ready to move on, ask him to give you a particular thing. Name the object and keep prompting until he picks it up. Carry on in this way. Don't worry if he doesn't always give you the thing you name. Just take what he gives you, name it, and thank him! Don't move on to this until you are sure your baby is ready. If he doesn't get it, try again a few weeks later.

WHAT TO DO:

1. Make sure your baby is sitting comfortably and well supported. Sit opposite from him.
2. Put the basket between you; together, have a good look at all the objects.
3. Take one of the objects and offer it to your baby. Talk while you do so, and be sure to name the object: "Here you are—here's a spoon. Can you take it?"
4. Encourage your baby to take the object from you.
5. Ask him to give it back to you: "Can you give me the spoon?" Reward him with praise and smiles if he does, but don't worry if he wants to hang on to it.

Another idea: Play this game at bath time with bath toys.

It's Your Choice
learning to point

WHAT YOU NEED:

- three small boxes with lids (shoe boxes are ideal)
- three small soft toys

Ready for more?

Play a memory game with the boxes. Ask, "Where's your teddy?" and encourage your baby to point to the box where she thinks it is. Put a picture in each box. Talk about the pictures, and then ask your baby to point to, for example, the cat, the house, and so on.

What is your child learning?

Gesturing is an important way of making yourself understood, and pointing is especially important. This activity develops the use of gestures and helps with linking language to body signals. It also leads to making choices and communicating them.

WHAT TO DO:

1. Place a soft toy in each box. Put the lids on and put the boxes on the floor. Sit down with your baby.
2. Show her the boxes. Shake each one to grab her attention. Invite her to choose a box. As she reaches toward a box say, "This one. You want this one?" As you say this, make a clear pointing gesture.
3. Open the box together and say the name of the toy it contains.
4. Hug the soft toy and play together; for example, give the teddy bear a drink, or brush the monkey's hair.
5. If your baby is just starting to point, gently take her hand to help her point to and touch the box of her choice.
6. Explore all the boxes, encouraging your baby to use pointing to show choices.

Another idea: Put a hat, a glove, and a shoe in the boxes. Put on the one that's chosen.

DID YOU KNOW?

Research tells us that children learn to decode facial expressions and gestures before understanding language.

HELPFUL HINTS

Some children find pointing difficult. Be patient and help by guiding her hand. If your baby goes to a babysitter or daycare, tell her caregiver that you're working on pointing. If your child loses concentration, hide some bright interesting toys in the boxes.

Squeezy Peasy
using hands to explore

WHAT YOU NEED:

- a shallow bowl, a board, or a small tray
- squishy stuff, such as dough or cooked pasta

Ready for more?

Offer a simple implement (a plastic brick, a small ball, or a reel) with which your child can bash the mixtures. Provide gelatin molds and plastic tools for your child to experiment.

What is your child learning?

Young children learn through touch, so allowing them to experiment like this is important. The more you talk about what you are doing, the better your child will learn to apply language to actions.

WHAT TO DO:

1. Mix the dough or cook the pasta where your child can see, hear, and smell what you are doing. Leave cooked items to cool.
2. Put some of the squishy stuff between you on the board or tray or in the bowl.
3. Encourage your child to reach out and grab some of the stuff with both hands. Join in the fun!
4. Talk about how it feels as you squeeze the stuff in your hands and between your fingers. Use words like *squishy, slimy,* and *smushy.*

A baby or younger child may bring the stuff toward his face. Don't worry if he puts some in his mouth. However, don't keep mixtures too long. Throw them away after use, and make some more.

Another idea: Add scented herbs (mint, oregano) to a pastry mix or dough.

11

Strings 'n' Things
making a tactile string

WHAT YOU NEED:

- laces or short lengths of wool, string, ribbon, or cord
- things to thread on the strings—for example, big buttons, beads, spools, or pieces of paper towel tubes

Ready for more?

Introduce some tins without lids (clean, with no sharp edges). Sitting babies love dangling ribbons into the tins. If you give her light chains, they'll make an interesting noise as they touch the tins.

WHAT TO DO:

1. Make some strings of things. Put one sort of item on each string—for example, buttons on one, beads on another. Work where your baby can watch you, and talk about what you are doing.
2. Put three or four of the strings in front of your baby—perhaps a string of beads, a piece of chain, or a few ribbons.
3. Watch to see what she does. Talk quietly as she works, encouraging her and commenting on what she is doing. Help if she needs it (she probably won't!), but stay near her and watch what's going on.

Another idea: Try ribbons and strings of different colors—see which your baby prefers.

What is your child learning?

Babies and young children love collections of things to play with. These strings of things will promote hand control and wrist movements. They will also encourage exploring and using language.

HELPFUL HINTS

This activity is better for babies who sit and crawl rather than children who have learned how to stand. Make sure the strings aren't too long. The child should be able to hold them up by one end.

DID YOU
KNOW?

Developing fine motor control of hand and wrist is essential for learning to manipulate objects.

Let's Dance
feeling security, showing affection

WHAT YOU NEED:

- some music on a CD, on the radio, or on an MP3 player (experiment with different sorts of music)

Ready for more?

"Dance" with a sitting child by holding his hands and moving them in the air (this will give you a rest!). A baby who is beginning to stand will love to dance with you holding his hands.

WHAT TO DO:

1. Pick up your baby or toddler and dance around the room with him, holding him close to your body. Hum or sing along with the music.
2. Make sure your child can see your face and make eye contact.
3. Some children love being swung high in the air in time to the music.
4. After a while, sit down together and take your child's hands in yours, following the rhythm of the music as you wave or clap together.

Another idea: Wave bells, a shaker (rice in a tin will do), or a bunch of ribbons as you dance.

DID YOU KNOW?

Positive interactions with caring adults stimulate a young child's brain and improve the links between brain cells.

HELPFUL HINTS

You can dance with a child in a cart or a wheelchair. Some children don't like being moved rapidly. Start gently and slowly with relaxed music. Children enjoy doing this with others. Involve a friend's child or a brother or sister.

What is your child learning?

Music and dancing are great activities for making you both feel close, happy, and secure. Developing a sense of rhythm is an important part of child development and has a big effect on learning

Look Who's Here!
fun with mirrors

WHAT YOU NEED:

- a mirror
- a hat
- a pair of glasses or a bangle

DID YOU KNOW?

Children learn to talk by hearing words over and over again, attaching them to objects, people, and actions.

Ready for more?

Dab some yogurt on your nose and encourage your child to reach toward you and explore your face. Use a "no tears" shampoo to make some froth on a play mirror. Rub away the bubbles to see the reflection.

WHAT TO DO:

1. Sit beside your child in front of the mirror.
2. Make some faces in the mirror. Say or sing hello to your child. Smile and reach for the mirror. Encourage her to respond to the reflections by copying or reaching toward them.
3. Put the hat on your head and then tip it off slowly, saying, "Gone." Offer your child the hat to put back on your head or on hers. Tip it off gently with smiles and say, "Gone."
4. Do the same with the pair of glasses or the bangle.
5. Use words and smiles to praise her responses (copying, reaching, putting on the hat, and tipping it off again).

Another idea: Get a small plastic play mirror, and leave it where your child can find it and play with it on her own.

What is your child learning?

The "tipping off the hat" game will help develop prediction. Look for your child showing anticipation and excitement. Practicing words and facial expressions supports communication skills.

HELPFUL HINTS

For babies and small children, play the "tipping off the hat" game face to face before trying it in the mirror. Some babies and young children may need to be supported to help head control or balance.

What is your child learning?

Like baby massage, this activity will help bond the relationship between you and your child. It also helps with the idea of taking turns. Naming and describing feelings and impressions will develop vocabulary.

Smooth Operator
feeling hands and faces

WHAT YOU NEED:

- baby lotion or perfume-free moisturizer
- a shallow tray or plastic container

Ready for more?

Use perfumed massage oils instead of lotion (choose mild scents and reputable brands). Play together at bathing and then putting lotion on a baby doll.

WHAT TO DO:

1. Put some lotion on the tray or in the container.
2. Sit beside your baby or toddler.
3. Put a finger in the lotion and feel it between your finger and thumb. Smooth some on your own hand.
4. Encourage your child to touch and feel the lotion. With one finger, gently put a little lotion on his hand or cheek. Spread it out, massaging it into his skin. Talk about what you are doing. This will help him understand what he is feeling,
5. Then, encourage him to spread lotion on your hand or arm. Talk about how nice it feels.

Another idea: You can also do this at change time or after a bath.

DID YOU KNOW?

Close contact will now have a positive effect on personal relationships later in life.

Splashing Out
grabbing, feeling, and letting go

WHAT YOU NEED:

- small sponges
- a washcloth
- lukewarm water
- a plastic tray

Ready for more?

Put the sponges and washcloth in an empty plastic food box and help your baby to lift them from the box, squeeze, and then release.

WHAT TO DO:

This activity works well in the bath.

1. Soak the sponges and the washcloth in warm water.
2. Sit opposite your baby or toddler and offer the sponges one at a time.
3. Encourage her to grab the sponge, squeeze it, and then drop it onto the tray.
4. Play alongside your baby, squeezing and dropping the sponge onto the tray.
5. Share the fun with smiles and say, "Drip, drip"; when the sponge has been dropped, say and gesture, "Gone."
6. Do the same with the washcloth.

Another idea: Add some "no tears" shampoo to the warm water and make bubbles.

HELPFUL HINTS

Allow your child plenty of time to explore. Younger children may not immediately reach for the sponges. Gently squeeze the warm water on to the back of her hand to encourage her.

What is your child learning?

Gripping and holding have to be learned. Picking up and releasing the sponges and washcloth will encourage fine control of fingers and thumbs.

DID YOU KNOW?

Developing fine motor control of hand and wrist is essential for learning to manipulate objects.

Look There
distance pointing

DID YOU KNOW?

When your child points, he is asking you to tell him the name of what he is pointing at.

WHAT YOU NEED:

- soft toys (a teddy bear, a dog, a rabbit, a monkey, and so on) and/or dolls
- a selection of suitable objects—for example, a hat, a cup, a piece of flannel, a mobile phone

Ready for more?

Play with a teddy bear and a doll, identifying body parts ("Where's your teddy's nose?" "Where's the rabbit's tail?"). Put everyday objects in a water tray to point to, name, and use.

WHAT TO DO:

1. "Hide" the soft toys around the room. Make sure they can be seen (maybe peeking out behind furniture).
2. Hold up one of the objects (for example, the hat) and give it to your child. Ask, "Whose hat is this? Is it your teddy's?"
3. Encourage your child to point toward the teddy bear (or whichever soft toy you chose) and then to put the hat on the toy.
4. Continue playing the game, pointing to and choosing a soft toy to give a drink, wash its face, speak on the phone, and so on.

Another idea: Hide cars, buses, and similar toys around the room. Play "Where's the red car?" to encourage your child to point to the correct toy.

HELPFUL HINTS

If your child finds distance pointing difficult, practice plenty of touch pointing first. Use pointing and natural gestures regularly as you talk to your baby or young child.

What is your child learning?

This activity will help in combining words and gestures, which is important for communicating. It will also develop using words to name objects and describe actions.

1–2–3, Clap with Me
a counting song

WHAT YOU NEED:

No equipment is needed for this activity. All you need is this rhyme:

1-2-3, clap with me,
1-2-3, tap your knee,
1-2-3, clap some more,
On your head and on the
floor.

WHAT TO DO:

1. Sit opposite your toddler on the floor.
2. Say or sing the rhyme and do the actions. Clap your hands and tap your knees, three times to the rhythm of the lines, and finish up by tapping on the floor.
3. Pause at the end of the rhyme and ask, "Again?" Wait for a look, gesture (such as smiling or waving), a sound, or first word intended as a request to do the rhyme again.
4. Encourage your child to copy your actions. Stop frequently to grab her attention.
5. Give your child lots of smiles and praise when she joins in.

Another idea: Take a teddy bear (or doll) and do the rhyme with his paws (hands).

DID YOU KNOW?

There are lots of websites with collections of excellent counting games and action rhymes.

Ready for more?

Vary the rhyme by doing tiny or huge clapping or tapping actions, whispering the rhyme, or using a funny voice. Put a few toys in a box. Count to three and tip them out.

HELPFUL HINTS

If your child needs help to start with, hold hands and do the actions together. If she finds it difficult to focus on this activity, use an exaggerated gasp or pause to grab attention.

Under and Over
hiding and finding

WHAT YOU NEED:

- a small blanket or piece of soft cloth (a clean dish towel will do)
- objects with different textures—soft, hard, bumpy, smooth, and so on

Ready for more?

Put the blanket over your head, gradually pull it down, and say, "Boo!" If your child enjoys this, put the blanket over his head and help him pull it off. Standing babies and toddlers will love this!

WHAT TO DO:

1. Sit on the floor with your baby or toddler.
2. Put one of the objects on the floor and name it as you do so (wave it gently if you need to get his attention).
3. Cover the object with the blanket, saying what you are doing: "I'm covering your teddy. Where has he gone?"
4. Encourage your child to reach under the cloth for the toy or object, or grab the cloth and pull it off.
5. Encourage and praise his efforts.
6. Try the game again with a different toy or object.

Another idea: Use a toy that makes a noise, moves, or plays music. Wind it up and put it under the blanket.

DID YOU KNOW?

Here and gone are key concepts for young children, who will need a lot of practice with them.

HELPFUL HINTS

Make sure your child is watching what you are doing. Stop and recapture his attention if he seems to be drifting. He may need help to guide his hand or to pull off the cloth to reveal the toy.

What is your child learning?

This is a cooperative game, so it contributes to the development of ideas of sharing and taking turns. Describing what's going on and naming the objects helps with vocabulary.

DID YOU KNOW?

Saying hello and goodbye are good ways of helping your child feel secure.

Hello, Goodbye
greetings and farewells

WHAT YOU NEED:

- a few play people, small soft toys, plastic animals
- a box (cardboard is fine)
- a square scarf or piece of material

Ready for more?

Get a few photos of family and friends and play "Hello, Goodbye" with them, putting them in the box and taking them out. Stand by the window and play "Hello, Goodbye" to birds, animals, cars, or whatever you can see.

WHAT TO DO:

1. Before you start, put a few of the play people, toys, and so on in the box. If it has a lid, close it, or cover it with the scarf.
2. Sit with your child in your lap or close beside to you.
3. Take the toys out of the box one at a time. As each one appears say, "Hello, bear," "Hello, firefighter," and so on.
4. When all the toys are out of the box, play together with them for a while.
5. When you judge the time is right take one of the toys, say, "Bye-bye, bear," and put it back in the box.
6. Encourage your child to copy you as you put the toys back one at a time.

What is your child learning?

This activity helps with ideas of consequence and order. Listen for the sounds or words your child uses. Praise new vocabulary or copying the words you use.

Hands Together
squeezing and pulling

WHAT YOU NEED:

- net fabric
- dry sponge
- small, soft ball
- hair scrunchies

WHAT TO DO:

1. Sit down with your child on a sofa, or the floor with older children. If he is younger, sit him in a baby chair.
2. Spread the items around, within easy reach.
3. Encourage him to reach for, grasp, and hold each item. Play together at squeezing and pulling them. Encourage the use of two hands together, pulling and scrunching.
4. Talk about what you're doing, and use words to describe the actions (*squeeze, pull, tug, grab, shake,* and so on). Encourage him to join in.

Another idea:

Try using some objects that make noises, such as a rattle, a sealed tin containing some dried peas, or a soft toy that squeaks when you squeeze it.

A Sight for a Song
singing about what you can see

WHAT YOU NEED:

- You don't need any equipment for this activity.

Ready for more?

Sing or chant about a photo. It can be a picture from a magazine, one of your child's picture books, or (better still) a family photo. Introduce some other tunes. Almost all nursery rhyme tunes are suitable. "Jack and Jill," "Three Blind Mice," and "Here We Go 'Round the Mulberry Bush" are useful. You could also use the tune from a current pop song.

WHAT TO DO:

1. Sit with your child in a place where there are plenty of things to see—at a window, in a park, and so on.
2. Begin to talk rhythmically about what you can see. Use plenty of repetition. For example: "I can see the mailman coming up the street. Can you see the mailman coming up the street? We both can see the mailman coming up the street."
3. As you talk, begin to tap on your knees or clap your hands to the rhythm of your chant.
4. Now start to sing about some more things you can see. Use a familiar tune, such as "Twinkle, Twinkle, Little Star." Here's an example.

   I see a blackbird in the tree.
   I see grandma's tabby cat.
   Can you see the blackbird in the tree?
   Can you see grandma's tabby cat?

5. Don't worry about trying to make the words rhyme (although you can if you feel creative!) or about keeping in tune. Just keep the song and the rhythm going.

HELPFUL HINTS

Hold your child's hands in yours and gently wave, clap, or tap in time to your song. Make up simple songs about what your child is doing to help her focus on herself and her actions.

28

What is your child learning?

This activity focuses on two important aspects of child development: developing a sense of rhythm (which has a huge impact on learning) and observing and talking about the world around us.

DID YOU
KNOW?
Children need practice in talking to somebody who isn't actually with them.

It's for You
taking turns with talking

WHAT YOU NEED:

- a phone (a toy phone will do, but a real one is better—mobile, cordless, or standard)

WHAT TO DO:

1. Sit comfortably with your toddler in your lap, on the floor, or on a cushion.
2. Show him the telephone and play with it, holding it to your ear and his ear, and pressing the buttons. Talk about what you are doing.
3. Put the phone down. If it has a bell, use this. If not, say, "Ring, ring."
4. After the ring, pick up the phone and give it to your child. Say, "It's for you. It's Mommy (or Daddy, Grandma, and so on)." Hand him the phone and encourage him to hold it to his ear.
5. Keep passing the phone to each other and saying, "Ring, ring, it's for you."
6. Model talking on the phone so your child picks up what to say.

Another idea: Let your child talk to someone they know using your own phone.

A Basket Full of Feeling
a texture treasure basket

WHAT YOU NEED:

- a shallow basket (a basket is best but a box will do)
- a selection of natural objects with different textures—for example: cones, shells, wooden spoons, brushes, natural sponge, wooden pegs

Ready for more?

Make a themed treasure basket; for example, a collection of shiny, hard, or metal objects. Make a collection of things from the bathroom, the kitchen, or the garden.

WHAT TO DO:

Treasure baskets are used a lot in nurseries to provide high-quality sensory play, particularly for babies.

1. Collect the objects and put them in the basket. It should be reasonably full.
2. Sit with your child close to the basket. She should be sitting so she can lean comfortably on the edge and reach the objects.
3. Watch your child as she selects and explores the objects. Don't intervene unless she offers objects to you or otherwise involves you. Use the time to watch how your child reacts to the objects and manipulates them with her fingers, hands, and wrists.
4. When she has been playing for a while, name the objects as she pick them up, and encourage her to imitate you.

Another idea: Keep the basket fresh by removing some objects and introducing others, but don't do this too often. Your child needs time to revisit several times before you make changes.

What is your child learning?

Exploring the characteristics of objects (shapes, textures, appearance, and sounds) is important in gaining knowledge and understanding of the world. Practicing naming them will help develop vocabulary.

Hand in Glove
making the most of hands

WHAT YOU NEED:

- gloves and mittens—wool, leather, fabric, whatever you can collect

Ready for more?

Make a treasure basket of different kinds of gloves and mittens. Put tiny baby mittens on teddies and dolls. Make some handprints with warm soapy water or fingerpaint on a large mirror.

What is your child learning?

This is an exercise in sharing and in exploring together. It will help your child learn to work with others (laying foundations for team work), as well as encourage him in tactile exploration.

WHAT TO DO:

1. Sit down with your toddler.
2. Put a pair of mittens on your hands and play at clapping hands, stroking your face with the gloves, and letting your child feel the soft fabric on his arms and legs.
3. Offer the mittens to the baby. Allow him plenty of time to explore. Talk to him as he plays, describing what he is doing and imitating his actions. Smile and share his fun.
4. Hold your hands up for him to pat. Sing as he pats your hands, "Let's pat hands together, pat, pat, pat."
5. Now do the same with leather gloves. Play Pat-a-Cake and other familiar clapping games.

Another idea: Try the game with household gloves.

DID YOU KNOW?

Clapping songs and games will help your child use both sides of his brain and help it to grow.

HELPFUL HINTS

Younger (and some older) children may not have developed the fine control needed for this game. For them, start with large, very easy-to-remove mittens. Some babies and young children may dislike some textures. Have a choice of different textured gloves. Respect their likes and dislikes while encouraging them to join in.

Follow That!
following a toy

WHAT YOU NEED:

- a wheeled toy on a string (a wooden quacking duck, a clicking crocodile, or even a skateboard with a favorite toy aboard)

Ready for more?

Toddlers love chasing. Tuck a ribbon or a furry 'tail' in your waistband and let her chase you! Put wind-up water toys in the bath and see if she can catch them.

WHAT TO DO:

This game is best for crawlers or walkers.

1. Sit next to your toddler and look at the toy together.
2. Get up and start to move away, holding the string of the toy in your hand.
3. Encourage your child to follow you. Talk to her about what is happening.
4. Go slowly, and at first, let her catch the toy very quickly. Gradually make catching a little more difficult.
5. Praise her effort and success. Keep playing the game as long as she is interested.

Another idea:

Play the game with a string and a bunch of bells, a shiny toy, a puppet, a few ribbons, some crinkly paper or a couple of plastic bangles.

What is your child learning?

This is an active game that encourages physical development and coordination. Chasing and catching will help your child develop confidence.

35

What is your child learning?

Children learn by imitating the actions of adults and the sounds they make. Grasping and releasing develop hand control. Filling up and tipping out will help them learn about the properties of objects, including containers.

In, Out, Tip it All Out
filling and emptying

WHAT YOU NEED:

- 10 or so everyday objects, such as a sock, a spoon, a washcloth, a bowl, a teddy, plastic keys, a board book
- an empty plastic tub or cardboard box

Ready for more?

Put some objects in a box and close the lid. Encourage your child to unpack the box, and talk to him about each object as he reveals it.

WHAT TO DO:

1. Sit opposite your child and offer him the objects one at a time to explore.
2. Show how the objects are used— for example, wipe the washcloth on your face and then gently on his face, and say, "Look, we're washing our faces." Encourage him to copy you.
3. Allow plenty of time for him to explore each object. When he seems to have finished, drop it into the tub or box.
4. Say, "Gone," as the object drops into the box. With an older child, use a complete sentence— for example, "The spoon has gone."
5. When all the objects have been put in the container, encourage your child to tip them all out. He'll particularly enjoy this bit!

Another idea: Use a pillowcase instead of a box.

DID YOU KNOW?

Repeating an action over and over again is called a schema. Children often repeat a schema for days.

HELPFUL HINTS

Some younger children find it hard to let go. Gently stroking the back of their hands will help. Some children become fascinated simply by filling up and tipping out—and this is all they want to do (sometimes for quite a long time!). If your child does this, it's not a problem; let him continue.

Fetch
pointing and vocalizing

WHAT YOU NEED:

- soft toys—teddy bears, dogs, rabbits, monkeys, and so on. (Pick your child's favorites.)

Ready for more?

Try the game with drinks, snacks, paint colors, and so on to encourage pointing and vocalizing. With older children reverse the tasks. You point or name, and they find the objects.

WHAT TO DO:

1. Sit down with your baby or toddler on the floor.
2. Set out two or three toys—too far away for the child to reach, but close enough still to be part of the game (a small mat might be helpful to make a visual boundary for the game).
3. Look at the toys and talk to your child about them. Name them together.
4. Ask your child to choose one. Get her to point to a toy she wants. Older babies may be able to name the toy if it is a favorite.
5. Praise her for pointing and/or vocalizing.
6. Pass her the toy and let her play with it for a while before asking if she wants another toy.

Another idea: Put out different colored plastic cups or plates for her to choose.

HELPFUL HINTS

Some children will need to touch the object before playing the game at a distance. If so, bring the objects nearer. As you touch or point to an object, say its name. This will encourage children to vocalize as they point.

What is your child learning?

Communicating choices is an important life skill. This activity will help your child learn to indicate her needs and wants. Using the toys' names also contributes to language development.

HELPFUL HINTS

Some children may find this difficult. Start with just two pairs; don't add more until you're sure your child has got the hang of it. Play the pillowcase game with items that make a noise. You hold up the object, shake it (or do what's needed to make a noise), and your child tries to find its twin in the pillowcase.

Two's Company
matching and pairing objects

WHAT YOU NEED

- pairs of objects: two spoons, two washcloths, two socks, two books, two toy cars, two cups, two small balls, and so on
- a shallow box or tray

Ready for more?

Put the pairs of objects in a box with a lid (a shoe box would be ideal). Shake it up, open it, and sort the items into their pairs. Put one of each pair aside and its twin in a pillowcase. Hold up an object and ask your child to find its twin from the pillowcase, without looking.

WHAT TO DO:

1. Put two pairs of objects (four things) in the box.
2. Allow your toddler plenty of time to explore the objects.
3. Hold out your hand and invite him to give you an object. Demonstrate how it is used, such as pretending to eat with the spoon or pretending to put on the sock.
4. Offer the object back to your child.
5. Play together, exploring the objects. Use single words to name the objects. Comment on the matching pairs by holding or pointing to both, saying, "(Child's name), look; they're the same."
6. Add more objects to the box or tray. Enjoy exploring the objects together, finding matching pairs, naming objects, and demonstrating how they're used through simple pretend play.

Another idea: Your child will love to tip out the box and fill it up again.

What is your child learning?

This promotes understanding of the uses and properties of objects. Naming the objects extends vocabulary.

41

Material World
in and out

WHAT YOU NEED:

- several squares of fabric, or scarves (try to find different textures, thicknesses, some opaque and some transparent)
- empty boxes and tubes, such as cardboard boxes, plastic tubes, or cereal boxes

Ready for more?

Play filling and tipping small boxes into a larger box. Try shells, twigs, and cones in small buckets. Poke ribbons or wool into, through, and out of small cups and cardboard tubes.

WHAT TO DO:

1. Sit next to your toddler and put the fabric squares between you.
2. Explore the fabric together, blowing, scrunching, wafting, folding, and so on.
3. Feel the fabric on cheeks, fingers, arms, legs, and toes. Enjoy the sensations together.
4. Talk all the time about what you are doing, using simple words to describe the fabrics and how they feel. Try to include *more, gone,* and *again.*
5. Bring out the boxes and tubes and push the fabric into them together. Encourage your child to try to put the fabric in the boxes, pushing and prodding, squeezing and scrunching. Pull the fabric out together.

Another idea: To make a change, try wrapping paper, tissue, cellophane, or foil.

What is your child learning?

This activity helps with observation and investigation skills, and it leads to the development of early concepts of shape and position. It's also good for helping to extend attention spans.

HELPFUL HINTS

Do the same activity with noisy toys, such as rattles, shakers, and a large cookie tin. Play "in and out" in the bath, putting objects into and taking them out of the water.

DID YOU KNOW?

Each game of hide and seekforms and strengthens thousands of connections between brain cells.

Hide and Seek
covering and uncovering

WHAT YOU NEED:

- a soft, thin blanket or piece of fabric (not too big)
- a toy that makes a sound (such as a fire engine with a siren, a musical box or top, a toy phone with a bell)

Ready for more?

Put the toy right under the blanket and help your child to pull the blanket off. More adventurous children may be brave enough to go under the blanket to fetch it, but don't force this.

WHAT TO DO:

1. Sit on the floor with your toddler.
2. Show him the toy, and let him feel it. Play its sound.
3. Put the toy on the floor (still making the sound) and cover it with the edge of the blanket. Keep it where your child can easily reach it.
4. Say, "Where's the (toy) gone?" Encourage your child to pull the fabric off the toy. Help him if he needs it.
5. Repeat the game. Stop when he has had enough.

Another idea: Put the object in or under a box, so your child has to lift the box or the lid.

What is your child learning?

The concept that something might still be there even when it can't be seen (object permanence) is a difficult one. This game will help its development. Reaching and uncovering aids physical development and fosters a sense of control, which is important for self-confidence.

Hey-ho, Here We Go!
active play and gestures

WHAT YOU NEED:

- a strong cardboard box
- a teddy bear, doll, or favorite soft toy
- a bag, a hat, or some keys

Ready for more?

Spread out some everyday objects (comb, pen, book, cup, TV remote, and so on). Name one and ask your child to find it and give it to her teddy or dolly. Make up some songs about the toys and their journey in the bus/box.

WHAT TO DO:

1. Set the teddy bear (or the doll or toy) in the cardboard box.
2. Sing to the tune of "The Wheels on the Bus": "Teddy on the bus goes brrm, brrm, brrm, all day long." Encourage your child to join in.
3. Invite your child to choose another toy or doll to go for a ride on the bus. Sing, "Dolly (or toy's name) on the bus goes bounce, bounce, bounce, all day long," and gently bounce the box up and down.
4. Give the child the hat and say, "Let's put the hat on your teddy." Sing the teddy-bear verse again. Repeat with the keys and the bag.
5. Use short phrases, pointing, and other gestures to help the child's emerging understanding of words, objects, and actions.

DID YOU KNOW?

Repetition of songs, rhymes, actions, and words strengthens the connections between brain cells.

What is your child learning?

This activity will help your child learn to combine words, sounds, and gestures to describe actions and make requests.

HELPFUL HINTS

If your child needs help to understand object names, use just two very familiar objects, such as the child's own shoe and a cup.

What is your child learning?

This is another activity that promotes choosing and naming. In addition, experimenting with these objects will help your child to process his observations of adult behavior.

What a Looker!
more mirror fun

DID YOU KNOW?

Social interactions with you and others help your child to process information, as well as to reason.

WHAT YOU NEED:

- a collection of hats (such as sunhats, floppy hats, helmets, swim hats, and so on)
- sunglasses, headscarves, hair ribbons, bows, scrunchies, bands
- a jewelry box with necklaces and bracelets
- a large mirror

WHAT TO DO:

1. Set this game up where you and your child can see yourselves and each other in the mirror.
2. Play alongside your toddler, allowing plenty of time for uninterrupted, unhurried exploration and play.
3. Talk to him about the different accessories and how they look.
4. Try some of the items on yourself. Encourage your child to do the same and also choose items for you.
5. Talk all the time about what you are both doing.

Another idea: Add purses, plastic money, envelopes, a briefcase, keys, a handbag, or a tote bag for more pretend play and dressing-up fun.

Ready for more?

Your baby or toddler will love unpacking your handbag and trying out the contents. An older child may pretend to be you! Can you get hold of a wig? If you can, it will add extra fun.

You and Me
simple pretend play

WHAT YOU NEED:

- a selection of real kitchen objects (such as a plastic mug, wooden spoon, metal saucepan, plastic whisk, metal teaspoon, plastic plate and bowl, and so on)
- bag or bowl

Ready for more?

Play this game with a selection of bathroom objects, such as a toothbrush, a comb, a sponge, or a towel. Keep a basket of real objects for exploring, filling, emptying, or pretend play.

WHAT TO DO:

1. Make a pile of the objects and allow plenty of time for your toddler to explore them.
2. Sit with her, talking about the objects and showing what they do; for example, pretend to whisk eggs in the bowl or to stir food in the pan.
3. Take turns putting the objects into the bag, one at a time until they've all been gathered.
4. Shake the bag and invite your child to choose an item. Say "(Name), look. You chose the..." Pretend to use the item she's chosen: "drink" from the mug, stir with the spoon.
5. Continue taking the items out of the bag or bowl one at a time, and play at using them.

Another idea: For a change try some simple in-and-out play, emptying and filling the bag.

HELPFUL HINTS

Some babies and children will need lots of practice imitating simple pretend play. Stick to just one or two very simple actions at a time. Humor will help to keep attention on the play; drop the cup and say, "Oh no! We spilled the drink," and hand your child a cloth to pretend to clean up.

What is your child learning?

This activity will help your child understand what different items are for and give her practice using them. It will also stimulate pointing and naming.

Choose Me a Story
sharing a familiar book

WHAT YOU NEED:

- three or four favorite story books

Ready for more?

Children love repetition. You can follow this activity again and again, using the same books and introducing new ones.

WHAT TO DO:

1. Collect the books and sit down with your toddler in a comfortable place.
2. Look at the books together. Invite your child to choose one for you to tell. Concentrate on talking about the books and letting your child have a real choice. Praise vocalization, looking closely, and making choices (even if they're communicated simply by pointing).
3. Share the book together, stopping to point to and talk about its contents, asking your child to point to characters and objects (and name them if he can).
4. If he is still interested, let him choose and share another book.

Another idea: Let him choose a rhyme from a simple nursery rhyme book.

DID YOU KNOW?

Reading stories and sharing books with your child will help him learn to read for himself

What is your child learning?

Learning to choose is important to your child's developing brain. By indicating control, he also develops confidence. Sharing books is essential preparation for reading.

HELPFUL HINTS

Some children, particularly very young ones, may start to choose simply by looking or leaning toward their choice. Some children find choosing hard to start with. Help by limiting the choice to just two things and holding them apart so a choice can be clearly seen.

Splash or Drizzle?
making choices

WHAT YOU NEED:

- a small sponge
- a washcloth
- warm water
- a small, shallow plastic box or tray

WHAT TO DO:

1. Place a few centimeters of warm water in the tray. Give your toddler the dry sponge to feel. Encourage her to use two hands to reach, pat, grasp and squeeze the sponge.
2. Drop the sponge in the warm water. Play at squeezing the warm water over your c hild's fingers.
3. Give her the dry cloth. Scrunch it up in a ball and encourage her to poke, prod, and squeeze it.
4. After a moment take the washcloth back, dip it in the water, and then offer her a choice. Say, "Which one?" holding up the cloth and the sponge for your child to choose what she wants.
5. Continue playing, offering choices and having fun splashing and drizzling the water.

Ready for more?

Use a tin lid or metal tray. The water will make a great sound as it hits the metal! This is a good game for outside in the summer. Have wet cloths and sponges in a bucket for your child to wring out, splashing or drizzling on a path or patio.

HELPFUL HINTS

Different sizes and shapes of sponges will help your child develop grasping skills. Dishwashing sponges with long handles are great for practicing reaching and grasping, and when wet, they are ideal for early mark making.

What is your child learning?

As well as practicing choices, this is a good activity for developing fine motor skills: grasping, holding, and squeezing.

What is your child learning?

An important aspect of this activity is for your child to understand your "give me" gestures and the simple words and phrases you will be using. Naming and identifying the objects will develop language.

Catch This
passing back and forth

DID YOU KNOW?

Learning a new move needs new connections between the brain and the body. Repeating moves strengthens links.

WHAT YOU NEED:

- a collection of small, familiar objects in a box or basket (a treasure basket)

Ready for more?

If you can, get together with another parent or caregiver and child. Sit in a group and pass the objects around, one to another. Young children find this difficult, so give lots of encouragement and praise them when they manage it.

WHAT TO DO:

1. Sit opposite your toddler.
2. Choose an object from the basket. Offer it to your child and encourage him to take hold of it.
3. Hold out your hand for the object and say, "Give the (object) to me, please." Encourage your child by touching the object to attract his attention. Wait to see if he gives it to you. Praise him if he does—smile and say, "Well done, you gave me the (object). Thank you."
4. If your child doesn't give you the object, touch it gently again and see if he releases it. Use your judgment to decide whether to take the object back gently and play the game again, or to try again another time.

Another idea: Try holding out another box or a tin for your child to put the object in.

My Hat!
practicing "give me" gestures

WHAT YOU NEED:

- several hats (the wilder the better! large, floppy, silly hats are great)
- a mirror

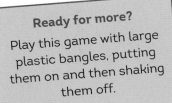

Ready for more?

Play this game with large plastic bangles, putting them on and then shaking them off.

What is your child learning?

Children need lots of repetitive games because they focus on anticipation and prediction. Being able to predict consequences is an important life skill.

WHAT TO DO:

1. Sit down somewhere with your toddler.
2. Put the hats in a heap and explore them with her. Put the hats on and play at tipping or pulling them off.
3. Next, put all the hats away except one. Give this hat to your child and ask her to put it on your head. Prompt her with natural gestures and single words.
4. Say, "Ready, set, go!" and shake your head vigorously so the hat falls off! When your child retrieves the hat, use an outstretched hand and words to ask her to hand you the hat.
5. Play again, this time putting the hat on your child's head. Show her her reflection, before doing "Ready, set, go!" to start her pulling or tipping the hat off.

Another idea: Make up a song to go with putting the hat on and shaking it off.

HELPFUL HINTS

This can be a lively game! Make sure there is a soft landing if your toddler falls over as she reaches for things or tips the hat. Use pointing and natural gestures to support understanding.

DID YOU
KNOW?
Learning a new move
needs new connections
between the brain and the
body. Repeating moves
strengthens links.

What's That?
exploring everyday objects

WHAT YOU NEED:

- some small boxes and bags
- several everyday objects, such as a cup, spoon, towel, brush, shoe, sock, and so on

Ready for more?

Get two examples of each object. Put them in different bags or boxes, and hunt for pairs.

WHAT TO DO:

1. Place two or three of the objects in each box or bag.
2. Sit somewhere with your toddler.
3. Play together exploring the boxes and bags. Name each object, but also talk about how it feels, looks, and how you use it. Use simple single words and two- or three-word phrases. Use lots of natural gestures.
4. Demonstrate the use of the object, such as pretending to brush your hair with the brush, and so on. Invite your child to copy your actions.
5. Allow plenty of time for unhurried, uninterrupted exploration.

Another idea: Play again, choosing some objects that are less familiar to your child, such as a key, pen, gloves, nailbrush, egg cup, whisk, and so on.

DID YOU KNOW?

Children who experience and understand simple routines will feel much more confident and secure.

HELPFUL HINTS

You might need to start with just two or three objects of particular interest to your child and build up from there. You can help him develop an understanding of routines by giving him an object, such as a spoon to hold just before a meal, or perhaps his coat to feel just before he goes out.

What is your child learning?

This activity helps with understanding objects and what they do. It promotes listening and encourages first words. It provides a starter for simple pretend play.

What is your child learning?

This activity will help your child practice using fingers, fists, palms, and wrists as she works. This is important in developing the hand control she will need later for writing.

Saucy!
simple food play

DID YOU KNOW?

Providing a rich environment that offers lots of sensory experiences stimulates brain growth.

WHAT YOU NEED:

- tomato ketchup or pasta sauce
- a tabletop or baby chair with a tray

Ready for more?

Let your child make patterns on a large sheet of paper (remnants of wallpaper rolls are ideal for this).

WHAT TO DO:

This gets messy, so you might want to put some floor covering down!

1. It is easier if your toddler is in a high chair, but you could just let her stand at the table. Make sure she is well covered with a big bib or apron.
2. Squeeze or spoon some tomato ketchup or pasta sauce onto the tray in front of her. Let her watch you do this.
3. Start experimenting with the ketchup, spreading, smearing, poking, and patting it on the surface. Encourage her to join in.
4. Work alongside her, modeling how you can use one finger to spread, poke, and make marks in the ketchup.
5. Try making some handprints.

Another idea: Try the same activity with smooth, soft, mashed potato.

DID YOU KNOW?

Connections between neurons in the brain that combine sight and fine motor skills help eye-hand coordination.

In a Hole
starting on threading

WHAT YOU NEED:

- the post from a stacking toy (if you don't have one, use a paper towel holder)
- bangles, hair scrunchies—anything with a large hole in it
- lengths of ribbon or yarn

WHAT TO DO:

1. Tie the lengths of ribbon or yarn to make circles or loops.
2. Sit on the floor opposite your toddler and put all the bangles, scrunchies, and ribbon bracelets between you.
3. Explore these together, rolling, spinning, tapping, feeling, smelling, and peeking though.
4. Put the bangles on your wrist for your child to pull off. Encourage him to try them on his own hands.
5. Place the bangles and other items over the stacking toy post. Drop them on one at a time,and take turns with your child to take them off, all together or one at a time.

Another idea: Hold a wooden spoon so your child can thread the bangles and other things on the handle.

Ready for more?

Play a taking-turns game, taking turns to choose an item and drop it on the post. Try putting socks on each other's hands and pulling them off again.

What is your child learning?

Threading and unthreading the items is a problem, and solving it requires your child to think and act on his thoughts. It also helps the development of fine motor skills.

HELPFUL HINTS

Some babies and children find using two hands together difficult. Make sure that if he needs it, he is well supported, so he can focus on reaching. As an outdoor alternative, try a bigger version of the game, placing rings over play traffic cones or posts hammered into a lawn.

Paint It!
exploring paint on a vertical surface

WHAT YOU NEED:

- some plastic sheeting (as thick as you can find)
- fingerpaint (it needs to be paint sold for children to use—don't be tempted to use decorating paint)
- large brushes
- protective (or old) clothing!

Ready for more?

Introduce a second color. Offer her some sponges or brushes to use for spreading and marking.

WHAT TO DO:

This will make a mess, so you need to be in the kitchen where you can wipe the floor, or outside.

1. Pin or staple some thick plastic to a piece of board. Prop it low down, where your toddler can reach it. It's best if it can go all the way down to the floor. The bigger the surface, the better.
2. Put the paint pot on the floor. Start with a single color. The aim of the activity is making marks and experiencing paint, not painting a masterpiece!
3. Stay with your child while she uses the brushes to convey some paint to the vertical surface.
4. Encourage her to use her hands as well to spread the paint out on the plastic, making marks, spreading, patting, and smoothing. Talk to her about what she is doing as she works.

What is your child learning?

Standing up for this activity will help develop the sense of balance. Painting is a good introduction to early mark making and a stepping stone toward writing.

HELPFUL HINTS

If you feel you need to experiment, try this on a flat surface first. Remember, this activity is about mark making, not picture making!

This activity is hard, and your child may need to build up to it. Start by making choices between two real familiar objects ("Which cup do you want?" "Which book shall we look at?"). Allow plenty of uninterrupted time for your child to process the information and choose.

What is your child learning?

Being able to choose is important for self-esteem and self-image. Children need to learn how to choose through practice. This activity will also help with language development.

In the Box
making choices

WHAT YOU NEED:

- a large cardboard box
- a small cushion

Ready for more?

Build choices into your daily routines (such as, "Which T-shirt?" and "Which socks?").

DID YOU KNOW?

Children who have lots of early experience of singing and music will enjoy it for life.

WHAT TO DO:

1. Help your toddler to climb into the box and sit on the cushion.
2. Rock the box gently from side to side while you sing,

   Yankee Doodle went to town,
   Riding on a pony,
   Stuck a feather in his hat,
   And called it macaroni.

3. Ask your child, "Again?" Wait for a response. As well as listening for sounds, look for nonverbal signals, such as a glance or body language, and then repeat the game.
4. Next, sing, "Horsey, horsey, don't you stop, just let your hooves go clippity clop," and jiggle the front of the box up and down in time to the song.
5. Jiggle the front of the box and ask, "Horsey Horsey?" Then, rock the box from side to side and ask, "Yankee Doodle?" Pause to allow your child to think and make his choice. As soon as he lets you know he wants more, sing the song again.

Bendy, Stretchy
copying actions

WHAT YOU NEED:

- space
- lots of energy!

Ready for more?

Play "Copycat," copying your child's actions, such as patting or clapping, singing a song to describe these actions.

WHAT TO DO:

1. Find a clear space. If the weather is fine, you could go outside.
2. Start jumping up and down and encourage your toddler to join you. Try jumping together while holding hands.
3. Sit down and stretch out your legs. Tap your heels gently on the floor or ground. Sing,

   Stretch, stretch, stretch just like me
   I'm as busy as a bumblebee.

4. Next lie down and stretch out your arms over your head. Sing,

   Stretch, stretch, stretch, just like me
   I'm as tall as a tall, tall tree.

5. Sit up and play the game again.
6. Now, stand up together, bend down low and sing, in a deep voice:

   Bend, bend, bend, getting very very small,
   Stretch, stretch, stretch, getting very
       very tall
   Bend, stretch, bend, stretch, up
       and down
   Bend, stretch, bend, stretch,
       now fall down!

Another idea: This is good fun for a group if you can find other children and adults to join in.

What is your child learning?

This is a very physical activity that will help your child to learn about how her body moves. Copying and imitating make an important contribution to learning.

Let's Hear It For...
clapping and patting

DID YOU KNOW?

Speaking slowly and carefully to your child will help him distinguish individual words.

WHAT YOU NEED:

- You don't need any special equipment for this activity.

Ready for more?

Make some pat mats with different textures in ziplock bags for your child to pat and grasp.

What is your child learning?

For a child, bringing his hands together in front of himself requires control: this is a key stage in his development. This physical activity is usually accompanied by sounds and first words, so it plays a part in stimulating language.

WHAT TO DO:

1. Sit opposite your toddler on the floor, or sit together in a chair so you are facing each other.
2. Hold your hands out and see if your child offers his hands. If not, gently take his hands and clap them together, saying, "Clapping, clapping, we are clapping."
3. If your child is enjoying it, try singing, "Pat a cake, Pat a cake, baker's man," while you gently hold his hands.
4. Hold your hands out and let your child pat his hands on yours; or, get very close and let him pat his hands on your face. Praise his efforts at patting and clapping.

Another idea: A tin lid or mirror to pat on will introduce a new aspect to patting.

First You Put It In, Then You Get It Out
play with tins and boxes

WHAT YOU NEED:

- some tins or boxes (wash food containers thoroughly first and smooth out any sharp edges)
- lengths of chain, shells, corks, bottle caps, pebbles

Ready for more?

For a change, provide a purse and coins. Larger ones are easiest, so quarters are better than pennies.

WHAT TO DO:

1. Sit with your toddler during the whole of this activity. Make sure she is well balanced and can reach the objects.
2. Allow plenty of time for her to explore the tins and objects.
3. Most children need no instructions and will immediately begin to fill and empty the tins.
4. If she needs help, just show her once, or play alongside her with your own collection of tins and objects.
5. Let your child play for as long as she wants. Some children will play for a long time! Keep watching her to ensure she's safe.

DID YOU KNOW?

Playing with "found" or recycled objects will encourage your child to think more creatively than store-bought toys.

HELPFUL HINTS

Check the objects to make sure your child can handle them easily to put them in a tin or box. They need to be small enough to go easily into the boxes, but not so small they're hard to handle. If your child automatically puts objects in her mouth (and many do), you will need to choose carefully what you're going to give her to play with.

What is your child learning?

This activity is good for promoting concentration. It also develops fine motor movements.

What is your child learning?

As well as being a lot of fun, this activity is good for developing hand control and spatial awareness. Children are often not aware of the space behind them, and this will encourage turning and looking around.

Spread It Around
painting around yourself

WHAT YOU NEED:

- large sheets of paper, cardstock, or anything that will take paint
- scissors or a sharp knife
- paint (suitable for children—not decorator's paint)
- a large decorator's brush

Ready for more?

You can do this outside on the patio. Just chalk a circle for your child to sit in and let him paint directly on to the stones. The rain will wash it away.

WHAT TO DO:

This activity is messy but your child will really like it! You need to be in a place where mess doesn't matter or where the floor can be cleaned.

DID YOU KNOW?

Paintbrushes are among the first tools your child will use. Early experience of tools will help with school activities.

1. Get a large sheet of paper or cardstock, the biggest you can find. You can get two suitable sheets from a large domestic appliance box, and you can use both sides.

2. With scissors or a sharp knife, roughly cut a circle 12"-15" across out of the middle of the paper.

3. Put the paper on the floor, and sit your child in the hole. Give him the brush, and put the paint where he can reach it.

4. Stay with him as he explores the paint on the paper all around him. Encourage him to turn around and paint at the sides and behind him, reaching out to the edge of the paper. Talk about the marks as he makes them.

Get It?
following and catching

WHAT YOU NEED:

- a small rolling toy, such as a wind-up car, a small toy with wheels, or a small soft ball

Ready for more?

Play the game with a toy on a string, pulling it behind you so your child can crawl or walk and catch. Keep close, don't go too fast, and stop when she is tired. Get her to pull the toy. She'll love being chased!

WHAT TO DO:

This game is suitable for a child who is just beginning to crawl or is already on the move.

1. Collect some small wheeled or moving toys. Sit on the floor with your child. You could be outside if the weather allows.
2. Show your child the toys you have selected, and look at the toys with her.
3. Now roll the toy away from you both and say "(child's name)—Get it!" Use her name as you point to the moving toy.
4. As she moves towards the toy, encourage her with words and gestures.
5. When your child reaches the toy, say, "Good try! Can you bring it back?" Praise her when she brings the toy back to you to play the game again, but don't worry if she doesn't! Just go and join her where she is and start again.

Another idea: Play the game with waterproof, floating toys in a plastic bin or in the bath!

HELPFUL HINTS

Don't roll the toy too far away. Your toddler may need you to demonstrate how to play. If she finds it difficult, try it first with a toy on a string that she can follow.

What is your child learning?

This activity has a sequence, so playing it will help introduce the ideas of order and of one action following another. It will also help her learn to recognize, respond to, and use words and short phrases.

DID YOU KNOW?

Watching moving toys and objects will strengthen the muscles in your child's eyes.

What is your child learning?

Pointing can be an invaluable tool for children as they learn to communicate, so it needs to be encouraged. This activity will also help with learning and understanding words and phrases, particularly the names for parts of the body.

DID YOU KNOW?

Fetching an object or article of clothing is much more difficult than just pointing or naming. Take it slowly!

Dress-Up Dolly
pointing and choosing

WHAT YOU NEED:

- shoes, hat, socks, gloves (baby clothes are really useful for doll dressing)
- a large soft toy or doll

Ready for more?

Practice isolating index fingers by pressing and squashing single pieces of cereal.

WHAT TO DO:

1. Play at dressing and undressing the toy or doll together. Talk about each item of clothing, and encourge your child to show you where it goes.

2. Encourage your child to touch or point to different body parts on the toy or doll. Say, "Look, here's a hat. Where does this go?" If he indicates by word or gesture where it goes, reward him with smiles and praise. If not, say, "On dolly's head!" and put it there.

3. Now take one of the items and say, "Can you put it over there?" pointing to a chair or table a yard or so away. Encourage him to look where you are pointing and help you put the item of clothing there. Continue until the hat, shoes, gloves, and socks are all about one yard away, but in different directions.

4. Now the idea is to find all the items. Ask your child, "Where are the gloves?" Wait to see if he indicates or fetches them. If he needs help, point to the gloves and say, "Gloves! Let's put them on dolly."

Another idea: Play with some other collections of objects, such as the things needed for a meal—spoon and fork, plate, and cup.

HELPFUL HINTS

Some children find pointing to make a request or share some information with another person very difficult. If this is the case with your child, be patient and reward him with praise and smiles when he begins to do it. Choosing can also be a problem, so give him help if he needs it.

Funny Bunny
making up rhyming words

WHAT YOU NEED:

- a collection of small soft toys
- a quiet place on the carpet or on a sofa

Ready for more?

Play together with a pop-up toy or a jack-in-the-box, sharing the anticipation. Encourage your toddler to play peekaboo games with you, holding her bib, towel, or other object and vocalizing.

WHAT TO DO:

1. Sit down with your toddler and the toys.
2. Look at the toys with her, picking them up and feeling them. Talk to your child about them.
3. Now choose one toy and introduce it. "Hello, (name), I'm Funny Bunny" (or Reddy Teddy or Soggy Doggy or Tony Pony, and so on).
4. As you introduce the toy, make it "walk" across the carpet or sofa towards your child. Keep saying the rhyming name as the toy advances. When you get to her, make the toy tickle her tummy.
5. Repeat the game with another toy.
6. Praise responses from your child, whether they're words, noises, or gestures.

Another idea: Use the rhyming talk as you and your child go through your daily routines. Don't use "baby talk," just rhyming words and names (such as, "Here's a shoe for you, that will do!").

What is your child learning?

Making up rhyming and fun names for things will help your child to develop her listening skills. Making up silly songs and rhymes helps children to vocalize. Sharing humor is good for bonding with your child.

HELPFUL HINTS

Encourage your child to make up her own names for toys and objects. Use pointing and natural gestures to gain her attention and encourage her to focus.

DID YOU KNOW?

The brain finds it easy to learn and remember rhymes. Pairing words that sound similar will help them to stick.

Here I Am, Look at Me!
swinging and singing

WHAT YOU NEED:

- some space on a carpet or other soft surface

Ready for more?

Sing some rowing songs such as "Row, Row, Row Your Boat," where you have to move together as you sing. Enjoy dancing together hand in hand or with both hands.

WHAT TO DO:

1. Kneel or sit with your child standing facing you.
2. Hold him gently but firmly under his arms.
3. Lift him gently up and down, in a rhythmic way as you sing:

   Here I am, swing with me,
   Up and down again, look at me.

4. Ask, "Again?" and wait for a word, wriggle, or look to indicate "more."
5. Repeat until he has had enough or you are exhausted.

Another idea: Play this game with your child facing you in a secure swing. Sing as you swing, then stop the swing on, "Look at me."

What is your child learning?

As he learns new songs and games, your child is learning to anticipate and concentrate. Watch him for growing confidence in new activities.

HELPFUL HINTS

This is a great game for encouraging eye contact. If your child is less confident, try swinging the teddy bear first. Let your child hold the teddy bear's hands.

What is your child learning?

Through frequent practice with this activity, your child will learn to recognize animals (and other toy figures) and their names.

What's in a Name?
playing a story

WHAT YOU NEED:

- a basket of toy farm animals
- a toy figure (such as a small doll) to act as the speaking character for your story

WHAT TO DO:

1. Tip the toy animals out on the floor or a table.
2. Spend some time playing with the animals with your child.
3. After you've played together for a while and your child has explored the animals, start to make up a story with her, using the toy figure as your main character. You could start by saying something like this:

   Here comes George the farmer. He's looking for his cows. He can hear them going moo, moo. Can you help him find the cows?

4. Continue the story, introducing each of the animals in turn and helping your child to find them. She may also like to make the sounds of the animals, put them in their pens or cages, feed them, say goodnight, and so on as the story develops.

Mine, Mine!
making your presence felt

- a digital camera or mobile phone to take a photograph of your child
- a way of getting copies of the photo (on your own printer or by taking the camera to a shop)
- sticky tape
- some large sticky labels
- a washable, chunky felt pen

Ready for more?

Get your child to make some handprints and stick them with the photographs. Attach photos of other members of the family to some of his things, such as Mommy's handbag or Daddy's coat. These aren't intended to be permanent!

WHAT TO DO:

1. Take five or six pictures of your child. You need photos that show his face clearly.
2. Spend some time looking at the photos together. Make sure your child can recognize himself.
3. With your child, use the sticky tape to stick photos to some of his personal possessions—high chair, trike, bed, changing table, clothing drawers, bedroom door, and so on—to the wall. Fix them at a height where he will be able to see them easily.
4. Say, "Let's write your name." Help your child to make marks on the sticky labels with the felt pen. The aim is for him to pretend writing, not his actual name. Stick the labels beside each of the photos.

The aim is to do all these things with your child, not for him.

Another idea: If you can find some fluorescent stickers, your child will love them.

HELPFUL HINTS

Really chunky markers are easiest for young children to hold, but make sure they contain washable ink! If your child doesn't seem to be responding to this activity, don't worry. He's just not ready for it yet. Put it aside and try again in a few weeks.

What is your child learning?

This activity introduces the idea of ownership (although it will take a very long time for your child to develop this). The starting point is for your child to learn to recognize himself and other people in photographs. It also provides practice in early mark making, which is a stepping stone towards first writing.

DID YOU KNOW?

The first word that most children recognize and learn to write is their own first name.

This or That?
making simple choices

WHAT YOU NEED:

- two simple snack items (fruit pieces, berries, carrot sticks, raisins, crackers, and so on)

Ready for more?

Give her a choice of books to look at together or toys to play with, always naming the choices and giving verbal prompts. Ask her to choose an activity ("Do you want to go to the park or play in the garden?"). Your child will find it much harder to choose activities because it requires a higher level of visualization, so introduce this later, and don't worry if she's not ready.

WHAT TO DO:

Your toddler may not yet be able to say "Please" and "Thank you," but turn taking and watching others' responses develops social behavior and a sense of occasion!

1. Put the two foods on different plates.
2. At snack time, offer your child a clear choice of food. Start with a choice of two things, and ask her clearly, "Would you like apple or banana today?"
3. Accept pointing or her own words, and help her thinking by commenting on her choice, such as, "You would like a banana; well done!"
4. Help her take her choice and prompt by saying, "Thank you." This simple procedure, followed often, will help your child to understand social language as you model the way to do it.

Another idea: Giving a choice of drink will reinforce the procedure.

HELPFUL HINTS

Your child may just point to start with, or she may begin to choose just by looking ("eye pointing") or posture (leaning/moving towards her choice). Accept this, but always put her choice into words yourself. Choosing is sometimes hard. Don't offer her too many choices at a time, or insist on her to choose if she doesn't appear to want to.

What is your child learning?

This is another activity that focuses on choosing. Your child needs lots of practice in making up her mind and expressing preferences. When she's around two, you'll probably wish she wasn't so definite! However, it's an important stage to go through.

DID YOU KNOW?

Crawling is a brain-building activity, make sure your child has plenty of room to move.

Your child might not want to go into the tunnel to begin with. If so, start with just one box and let him practice crawling through that first. If your child is a reluctant crawler, tie his favorite soft toy to the end of a string, and pull it slowly through the tunnel for him to follow. Help him out quickly if he shows any signs of distress.

What is your child learning?

This is a physical activity, which will help your child develop his body. It's also an exercise in exploration and problem solving.

Crawler Explorer
tunnels and dens

WHAT YOU NEED:

- large cardboard boxes
- a selection of small, noisy toys of different colors and textures

Ready for more?

Throw small cloths over the toys inside the tunnels so your child can peek under the cloths to find the toys. Encourage your child to crawl through the tunnels pushing soft toys or beach balls (such as, "Let's take your teddy bear through the tunnel.")

WHAT TO DO:

This activity is particularly good if your child is learning to crawl. It needs quite a lot of space.

1. Open the ends of the cardboard boxes, and push the flaps inside to strengthen the sides of the boxes. Use the boxes to make simple tunnels. Check thoroughly for any staples or sharp edges.
2. Loosely fix the cardboard boxes tunnels together to make a run. Put some of the toys at different places in the tunnels.
3. Bend down with your child to look into the tunnel and explore what's in there. Encourage him to peek inside, reach for the toy, and then crawl through the tunnel, exploring the different sounds, colors, and textures of the toys.

Another idea: Play peekaboo from one end of the tunnel to another.

Point and Poke
exploring holes

WHAT YOU NEED:

- things with holes— sieves, colanders, plastic tea strainers, plastic or cardboard tubes, slotted spoons, and spatulas
- canned whipped cream

Ready for more?

Help your child isolate her index fingers to make patterns in the cream or to poke into the holes. Spread sprinkles on a plastic tray and play at sprinkling the tiny strands.

WHAT TO DO:

This activity can be messy, so make sure that surfaces are protected!

1. Sit with your child at a table or on the floor.
2. Squeeze a small amount of cream into the colander or sieve, and explore it with your baby, pushing it through the holes, feeling the different textures.
3. Pat the cream with the spoons and spatulas, adding more cream as needed.
4. Sing or chant a simple commentary, using single words and short phrases describing how you are both exploring the cream and holes; for example, "Pat, pat, pat," or, "Push it in the hole," and, "All gone."

Another idea: Put some cream on your child's hands or tummy and sing "Round and Round the Garden."

HELPFUL HINTS

Some older children continue putting objects in their mouths well beyond the time that many babies and children do. Your child may be one of them. It's not wrong (children develop in different ways and at different rates), but be aware that it can happen. As an alternative to cream, try mashed potatoes (don't worry about waste; the garden birds will eat it when you've finished).

What is your child learning?

This activity will help your child to explore and understand objects and textures. Talking as you go will contribute to her language development, and you may find she will start to imitate you.

What is your child learning?

This activity will support your child's growing interest in role play.

Time for a Change
a changing table game

WHAT YOU NEED:

- plastic straws
- small paper or plastic plates
- color photos of faces cut from magazines
- glue stick or tape

Ready for more?

Use a slip-in photo album to make a collection of faces from magazines, photos of children making faces, clowns, masks, and so on. Use the book to talk through feelings, or let your child explore it on his own. Make up some stories using two or three of the masks.

WHAT TO DO:

As your child gets older and more mobile, changing time can be a bit of a challenge! These feelings masks may help to keep your relationships positive.

DID YOU KNOW?

Role play helps children understand the feelings of others and empathize with them.

1. Make some simple masks by sticking photos on the plates. Attach a straw to each, and keep them in a special tub or container near the changing area.
2. At changing time, offer the collection of masks to the child, so he can look at the faces and talk to them.
3. Sometimes, put one of the masks in front of your face and then pop out from behind it making a face with the same expression. This will probably result in much fun!

Another idea: Your child will particularly like the faces of other children, but it can be fun to try some animal faces, too.

A Family Affair
your child's own treasure box

WHAT YOU NEED:

- a basket or box
- objects of special significance to your child—her own washcloth, a doll, a favorite book, a comfort toy, your partner's or your gloves, a hat, a shoe, or a sock

Ready for more?

You can play this game over and over again, making a different collection of objects each time. If you have a digital camera and printer, take some photographs of the objects and play at matching the photo to the object.

WHAT TO DO:

Your child may have played with a treasure basket before, particularly if she goes to a care setting. This one is different—it's a collection of things personal to your child and your family.

1. Collect some objects for the basket. Ten or so will be plenty.
2. Give the objects to your child one by one to explore. Name the object and say whose it is: for example, "Look, Daddy's sock," or "Look, (name's) shoe." Mime or demonstrate the use of each object, such as pretending to put the shoe on the child's foot.
3. Next, encourage your child to place the object in the basket. Repeat with the other objects.

DID YOU KNOW?

The bond between a child and her parents is called attachment. It is vital for healthy development.

HELPFUL HINTS

Start with just two objects, and build up the number as your child becomes more confident. Talk all the time with your child about what you are doing, and repeat the name of each object lots of times. Use lots of gestures, exaggerated gasps, and pointing to support early understanding of these first words.

What is your child learning?

There are three main aspects to this activity: learning the names for things, learning or confirming their uses, and learning to associate an object with a person. It will also help your child with the concept of "mine" and "somebody else's" (although this takes a long time to develop properly).

Index